Riding with Paul Revere

By Holly Karapetkova
Illustrated By Pete McDonnell

ROURKE PUBLISHING

Vero Beach, Florida 32964

www.rourkepublishing.com

Edited by Meg Greve
Illustrated by Pete McDonnell
Art Direction by Renee Brady
Page Layout by Heather Botto

Photo Credits: © Soubrette: title page (bckgnd); © Library of Congress: pg. 4, 26; © peter zelei: pg. 4 (bckgnd); © Duncan Walker: pg. 4 (vintage paper); © Dmitry Knorre: pgs. 26-32 (lantern); © CCA 3.0 (Urban); © Heather Botto: pg. 29

Library of Congress Cataloging-in-Publication Data

Karapetkova, Holly.
  Riding with Paul Revere / Holly Karapetkova.
      p. cm. -- (Eye on history graphic illustrated)
  Includes bibliographical references and index.
  ISBN 978-1-60694-442-4 (alk. paper)
  ISBN 978-1-60694-551-3 (soft cover)
  1. Revere, Paul, 1735-1818--Juvenile literature. 2. Massachusetts--History--Revolution,
1775-1783--Juvenile literature. 3. Lexington, Battle of, Lexington, Mass.,
1775--Juvenile literature. 4. Concord, Battle of, Concord, Mass.,
1775--Juvenile literature. 5. Statesmen--Massachusetts--Biography--Juvenile
literature. 6. Massachusetts--Biography--Juvenile literature. I. Title.
  F69.R43K37 2010
  973.3'311092--dc22

                              2009020504

Printed in the USA
CG/CG

www.rourkepublishing.com - rourke@rourkepublishing.com
Post Office Box 643328 Vero Beach, Florida 32964

Table of Contents

The Boston Journal

Monday | Issue 1 Volume 4 | April 17, 1775

Parliament Continues Harsh Legislation

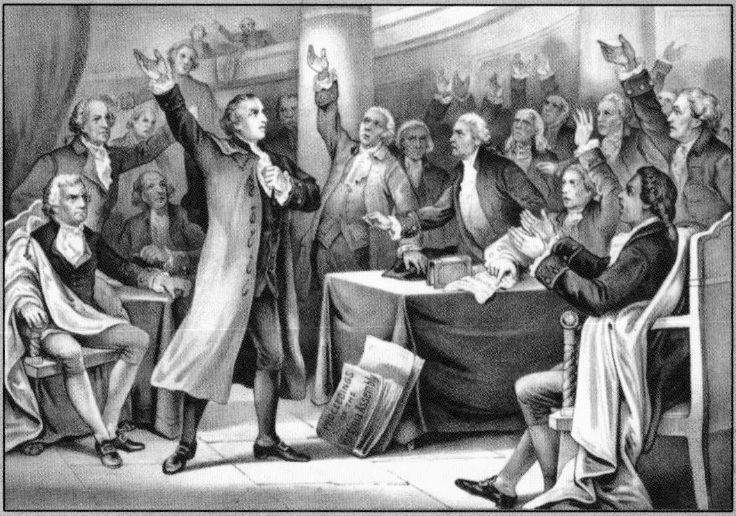
PROCEEDINGS

At noon today, the town crier gave the following notice throughout the town.

British Parliament continues to impose harsh legislation and taxation on the colonies. Tension is growing and many colonists are upset at the unfair treatment. They want a representative who will fight for the rights of the colonies. "No taxation without representation!" is the cry coming from the colonists.

"Give me liberty or give me death!" declared Patrick Henry passionately as he addressed delegates in Virginia on March 23. His words ultimately persuaded Virginia to join the rebellion. John Hancock and Samuel Adams openly spoke out against the oppressive British and are now marked men. Many have joined the Patriots and it only seems to be a matter of time before the real fighting begins.

The Boston Tea Party was in recation to Great Britain's harsh tax laws.

Before the United States of America was an independent country, it was a group of **Colonies** ruled by Great Britain. In the 1760s, the British Parliament passed a series of **tax** laws charging high taxes on a variety of items, such as paper and tea. The Colonies didn't think the tax laws were fair. They didn't have any **representatives** to speak for them in the British Parliament, where such laws were made.

The **Sons of Liberty** in Boston and **patriot** groups in other Colonies started to **protest** against the taxes. On December 16, 1773, the Sons of Liberty dressed up as Native Americans and boarded three tea ships in the Boston Harbor. They dumped 342 chests of tea into the water. Paul Revere was one of the Sons of Liberty and probably took part in what became known as the Boston Tea Party.

Tensions between the British grew and by April of 1775, the colonists found out that the British planned to arrest Samuel Adams and John Hancock, two American patriot leaders, and take military supplies stored in the town of Concord. On the night of April 18, Paul Revere rode from Boston to Lexington to warn everyone that the British *regulars* were coming. Thanks to Paul Revere and other messengers, the American **militiamen**, or minutemen, were prepared for the battles of Lexington and Concord, which were the first fights of the American **Revolution**.

No Taxation Without Representation

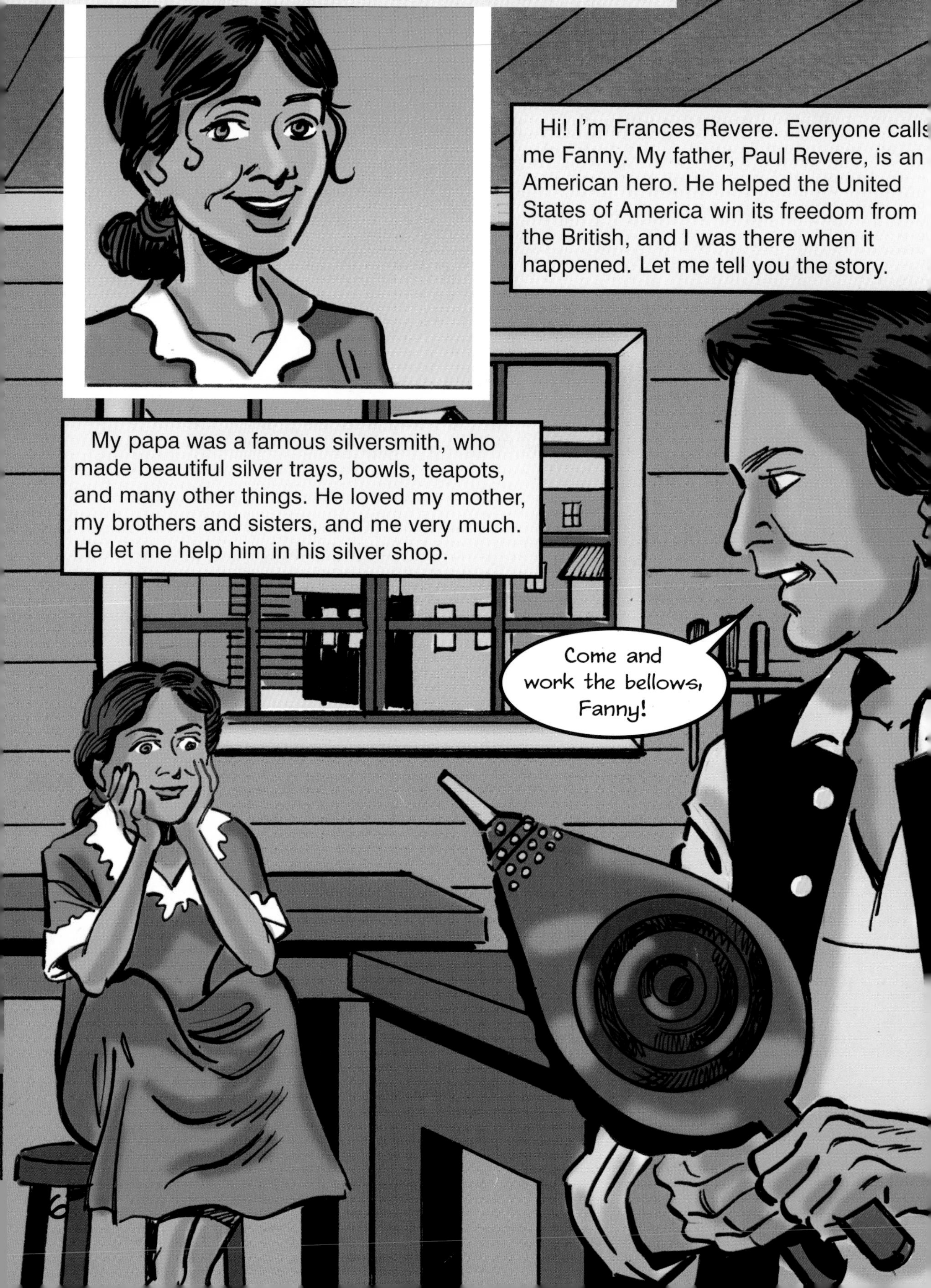
Hi! I'm Frances Revere. Everyone calls me Fanny. My father, Paul Revere, is an American hero. He helped the United States of America win its freedom from the British, and I was there when it happened. Let me tell you the story.
My papa was a famous silversmith, who made beautiful silver trays, bowls, teapots, and many other things. He loved my mother, my brothers and sisters, and me very much. He let me help him in his silver shop.
Come and work the bellows, Fanny!

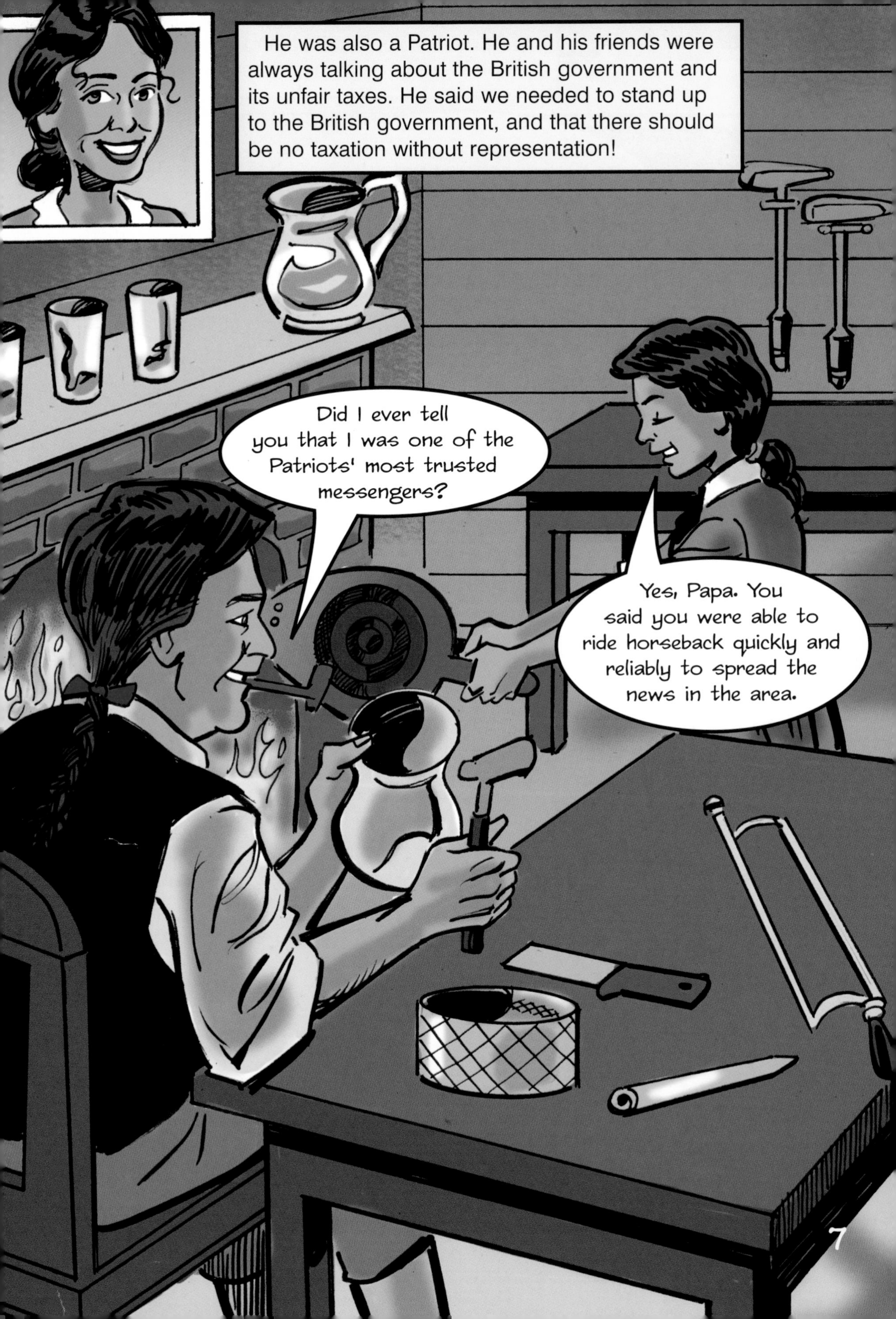
He was also a Patriot. He and his friends were always talking about the British government and its unfair taxes. He said we needed to stand up to the British government, and that there should be no taxation without representation!
Did I ever tell you that I was one of the Patriots' most trusted messengers?
Yes, Papa. You said you were able to ride horseback quickly and reliably to spread the news in the area.

The Plan

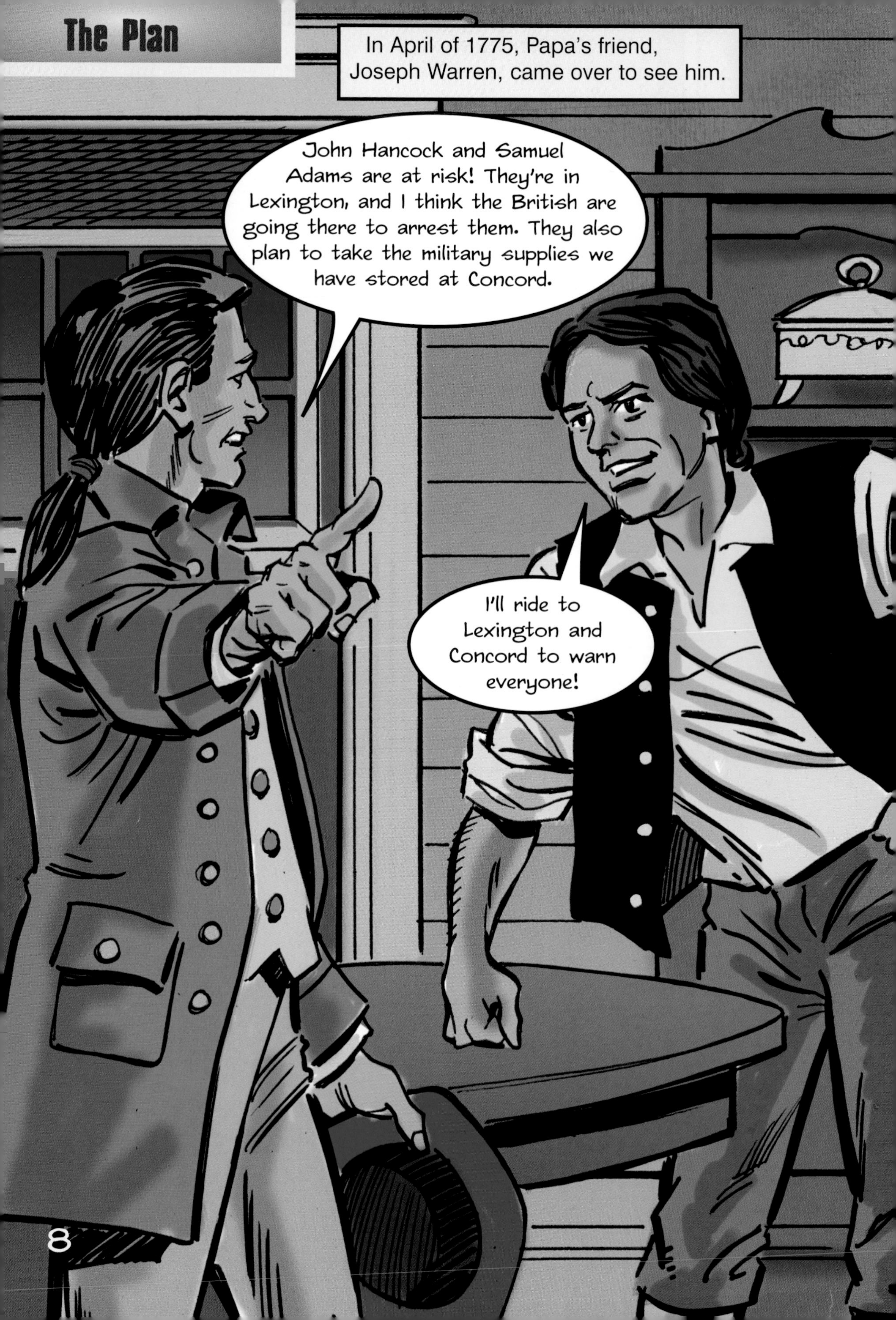
In April of 1775, Papa's friend, Joseph Warren, came over to see him.
John Hancock and Samuel Adams are at risk! They're in Lexington, and I think the British are going there to arrest them. They also plan to take the military supplies we have stored at Concord.
I'll ride to Lexington and Concord to warn everyone!

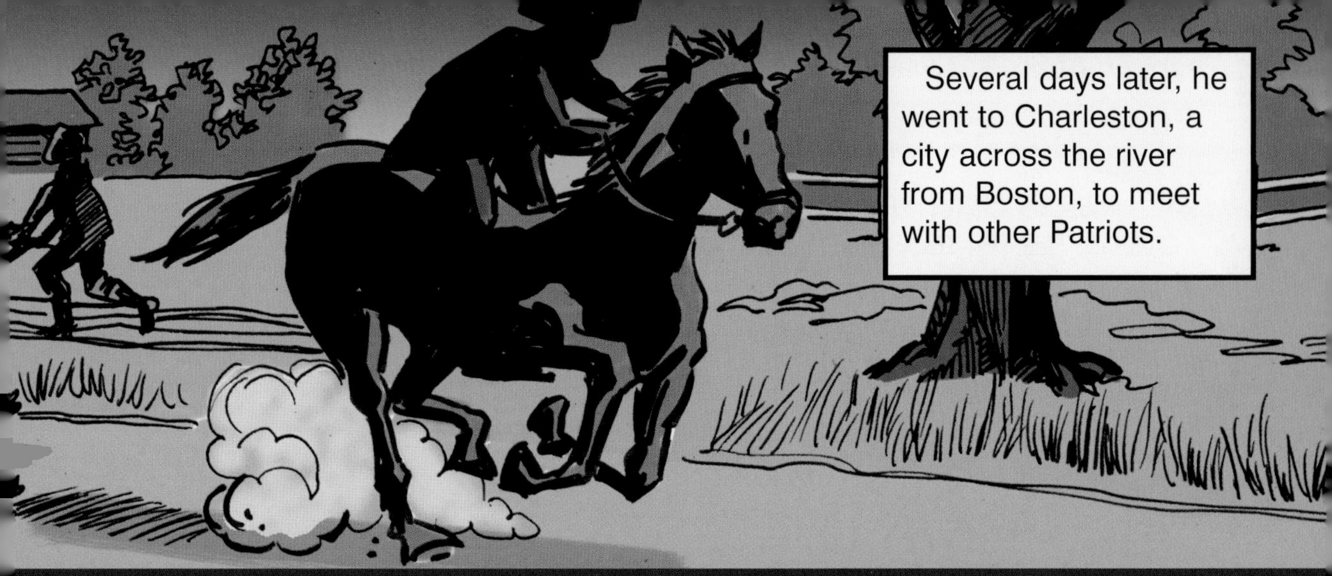
Several days later, he went to Charleston, a city across the river from Boston, to meet with other Patriots.

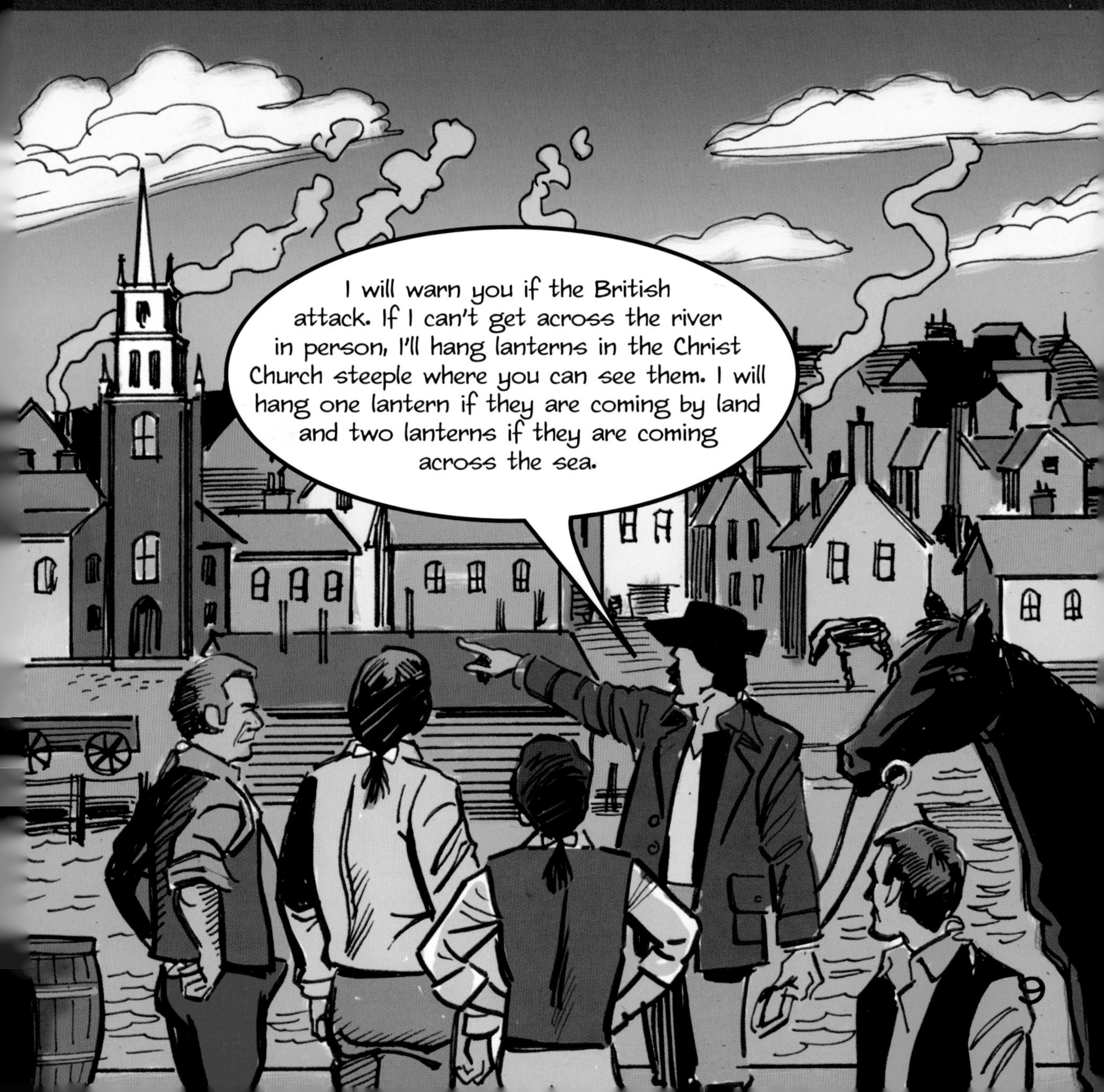
I will warn you if the British attack. If I can't get across the river in person, I'll hang lanterns in the Christ Church steeple where you can see them. I will hang one lantern if they are coming by land and two lanterns if they are coming across the sea.

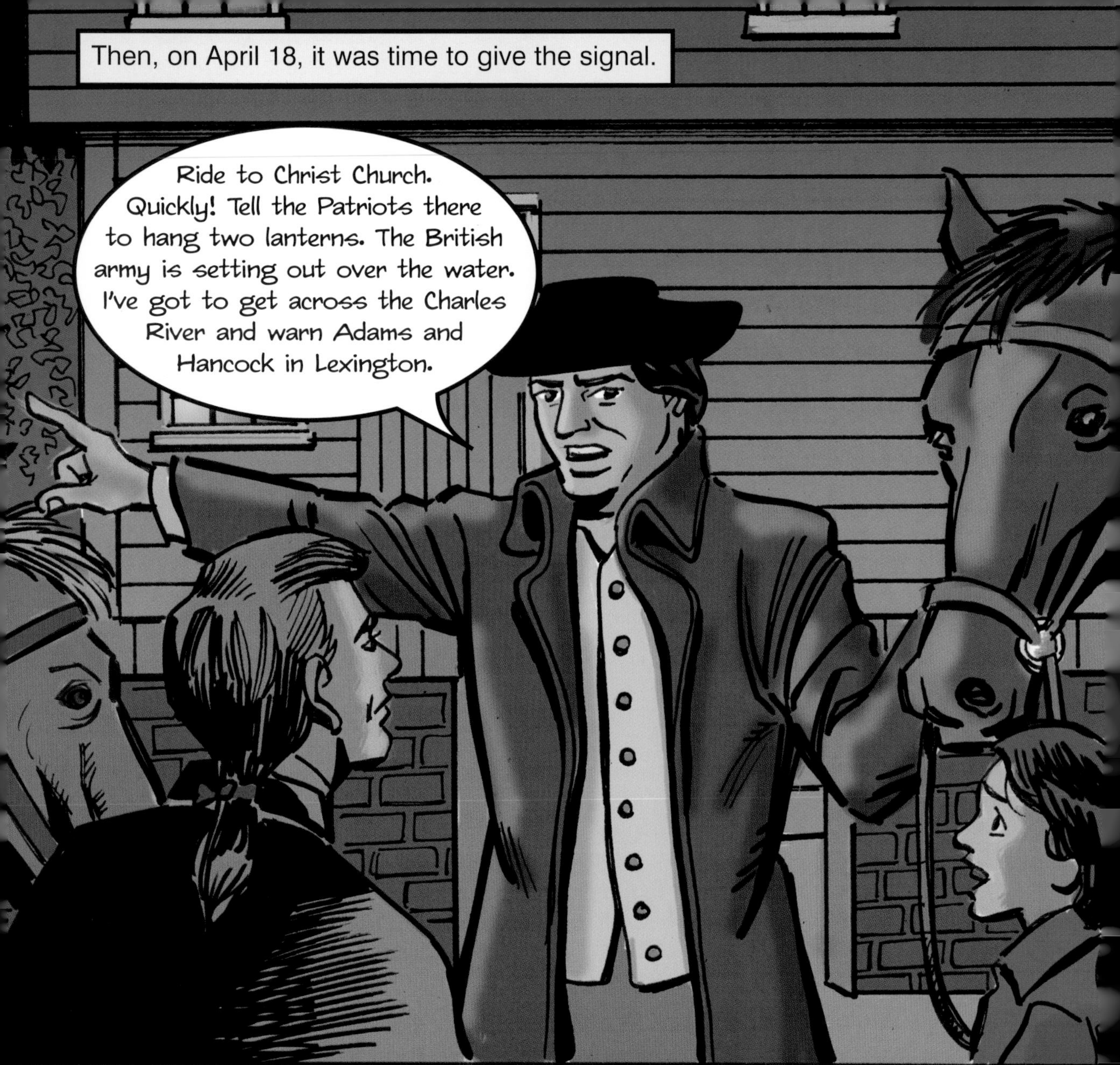
Then, on April 18, it was time to give the signal.
Ride to Christ Church. Quickly! Tell the Patriots there to hang two lanterns. The British army is setting out over the water. I've got to get across the Charles River and warn Adams and Hancock in Lexington.

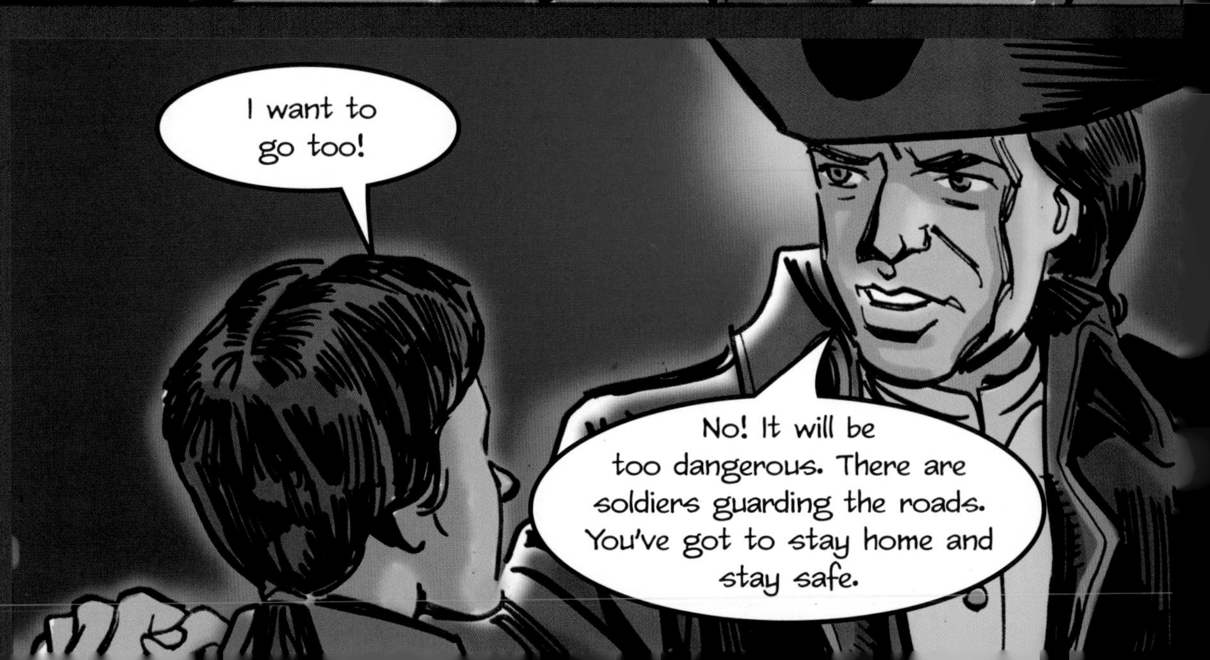
I want to go too!
No! It will be too dangerous. There are soldiers guarding the roads. You've got to stay home and stay safe.

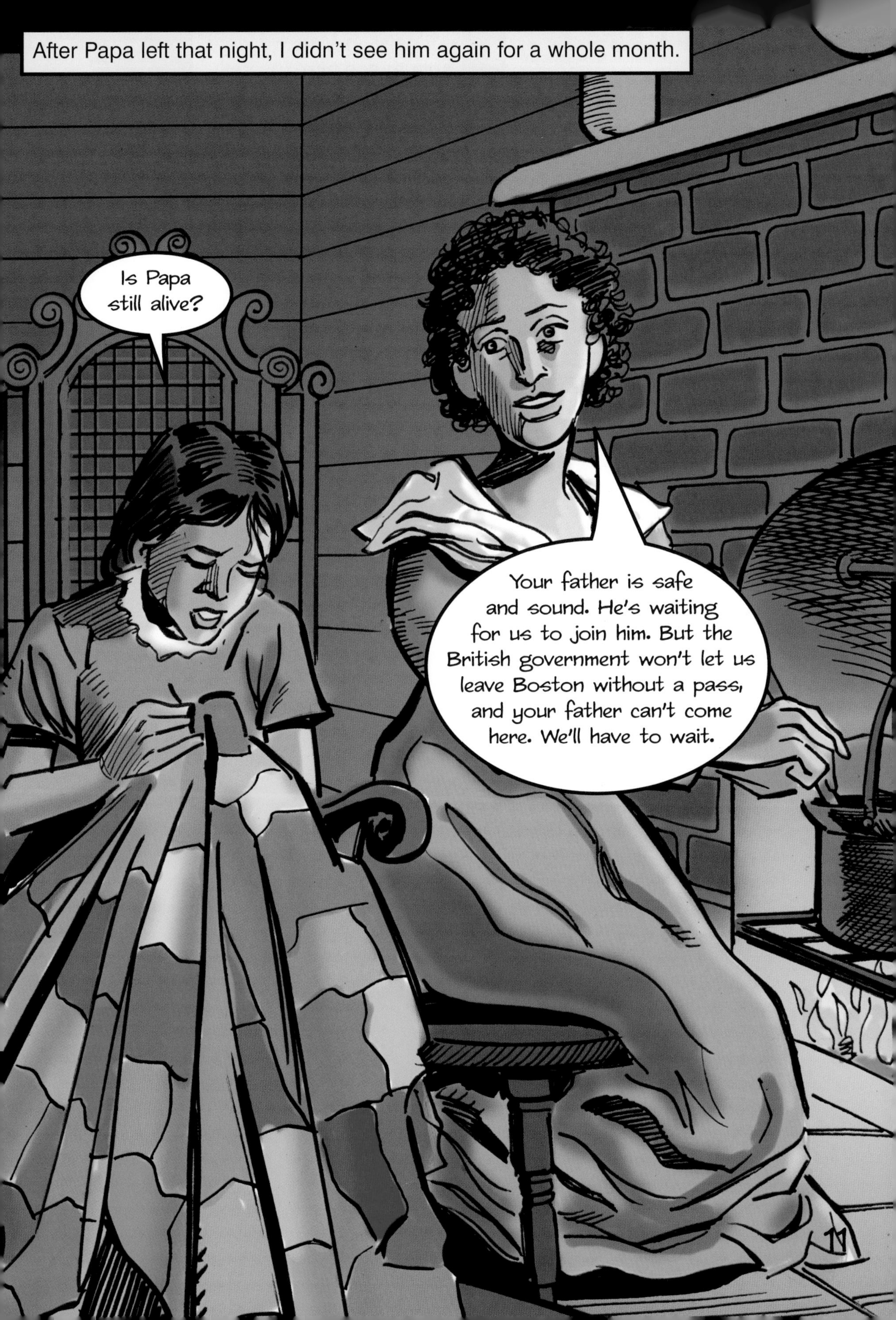
After Papa left that night, I didn't see him again for a whole month.
Is Papa still alive?
Your father is safe and sound. He's waiting for us to join him. But the British government won't let us leave Boston without a pass, and your father can't come here. We'll have to wait.

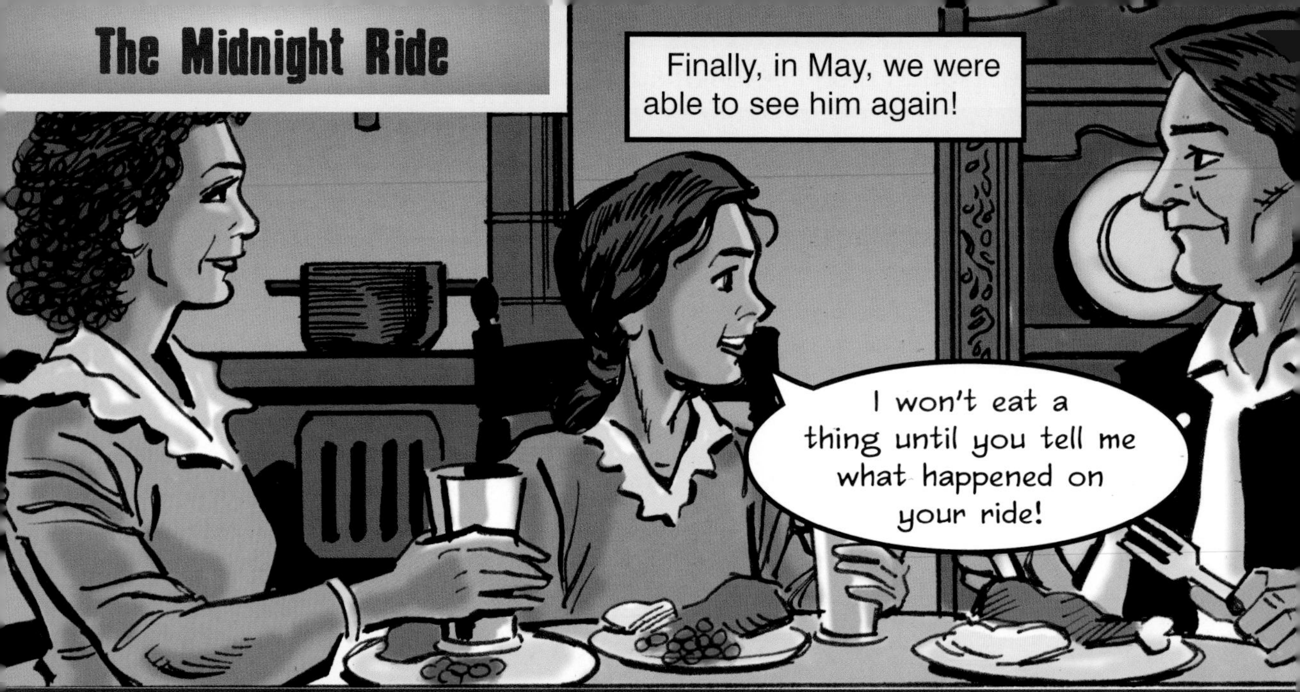
Finally, in May, we were able to see him again!
I won't eat a thing until you tell me what happened on your ride!

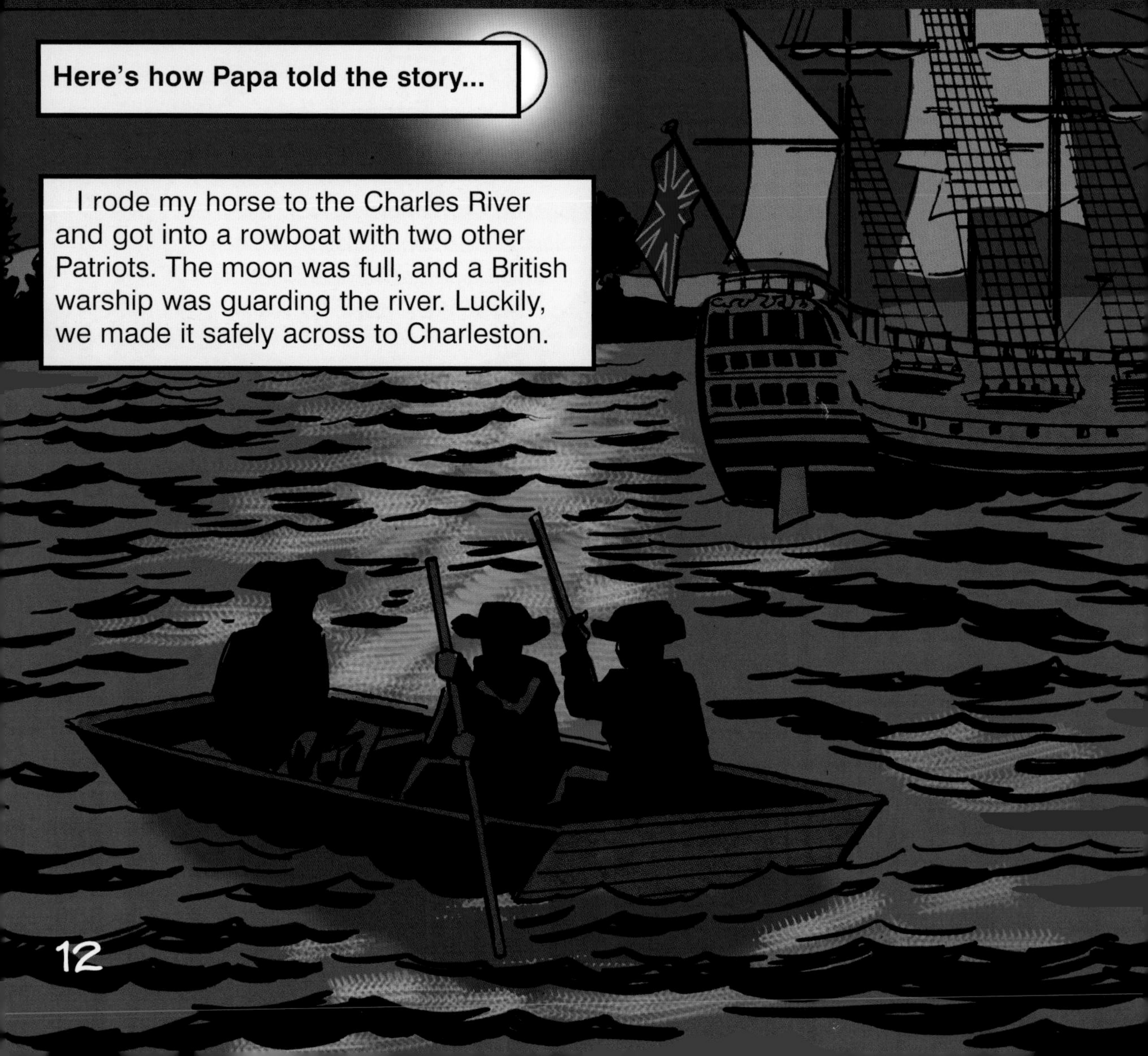
Here's how Papa told the story...
I rode my horse to the Charles River and got into a rowboat with two other Patriots. The moon was full, and a British warship was guarding the river. Luckily, we made it safely across to Charleston.

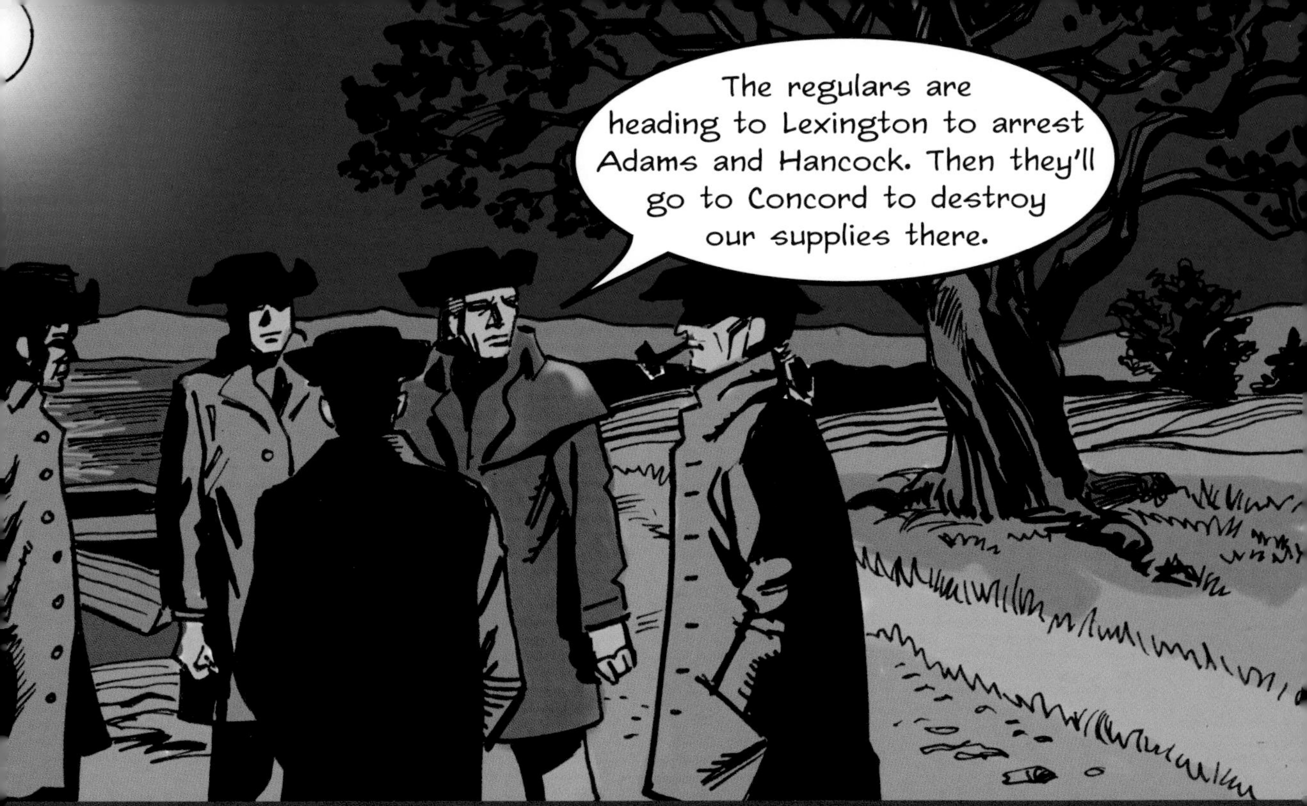
The regulars are heading to Lexington to arrest Adams and Hancock. Then they'll go to Concord to destroy our supplies there.

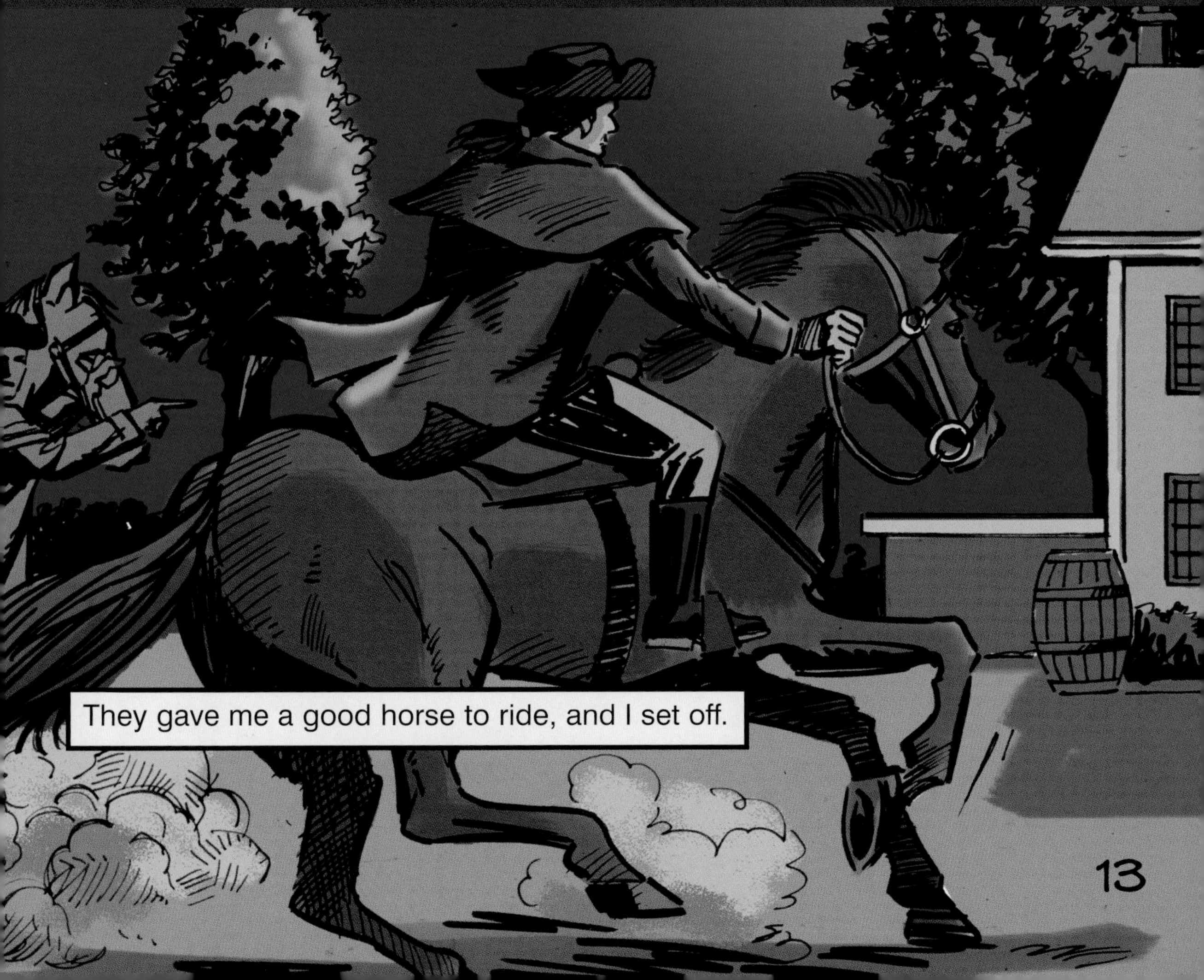
They gave me a good horse to ride, and I set off.

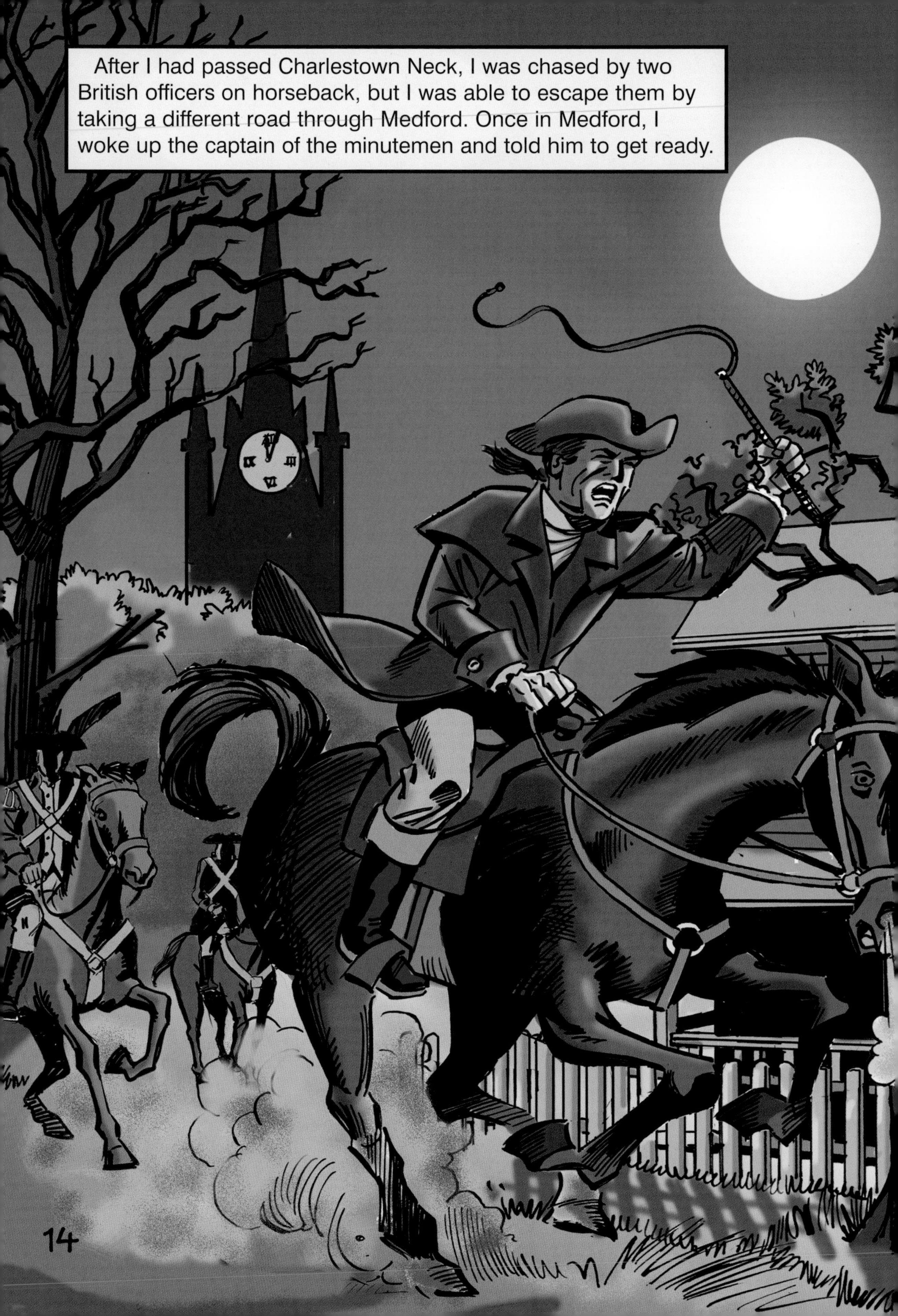
After I had passed Charlestown Neck, I was chased by two British officers on horseback, but I was able to escape them by taking a different road through Medford. Once in Medford, I woke up the captain of the minutemen and told him to get ready.

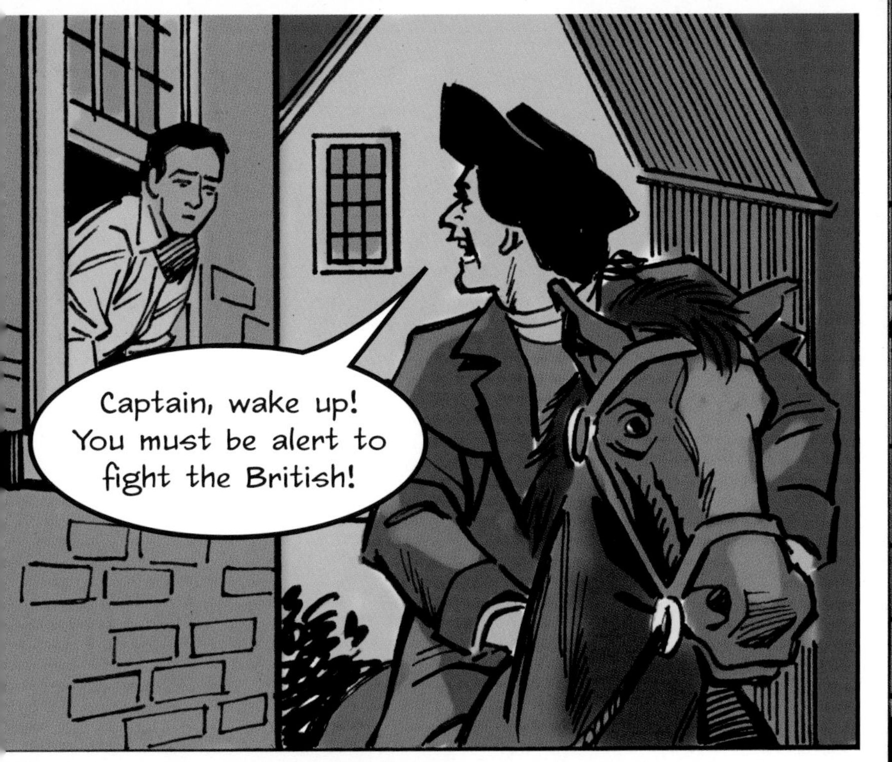
Captain, wake up! You must be alert to fight the British!

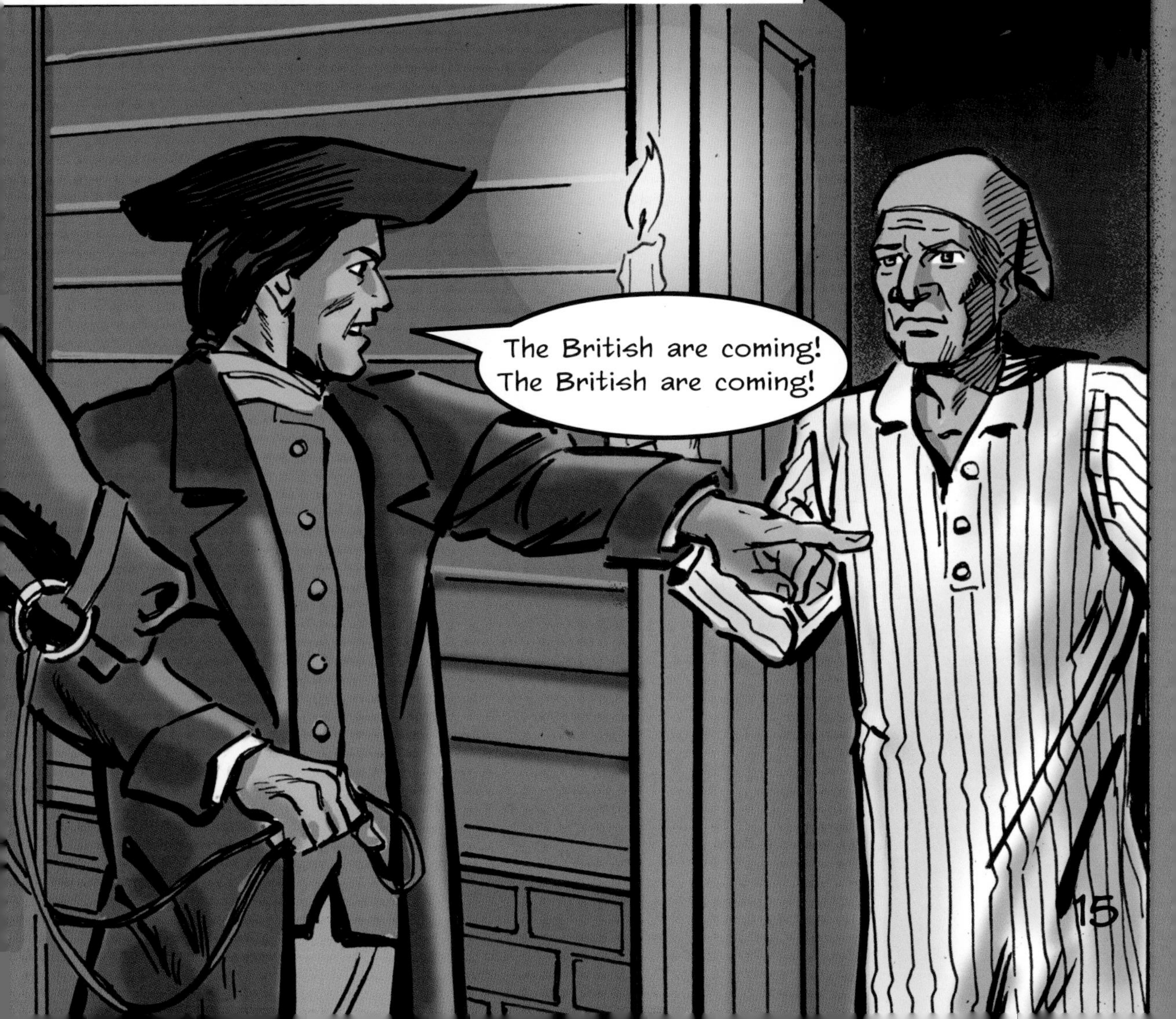
The British are coming! The British are coming!

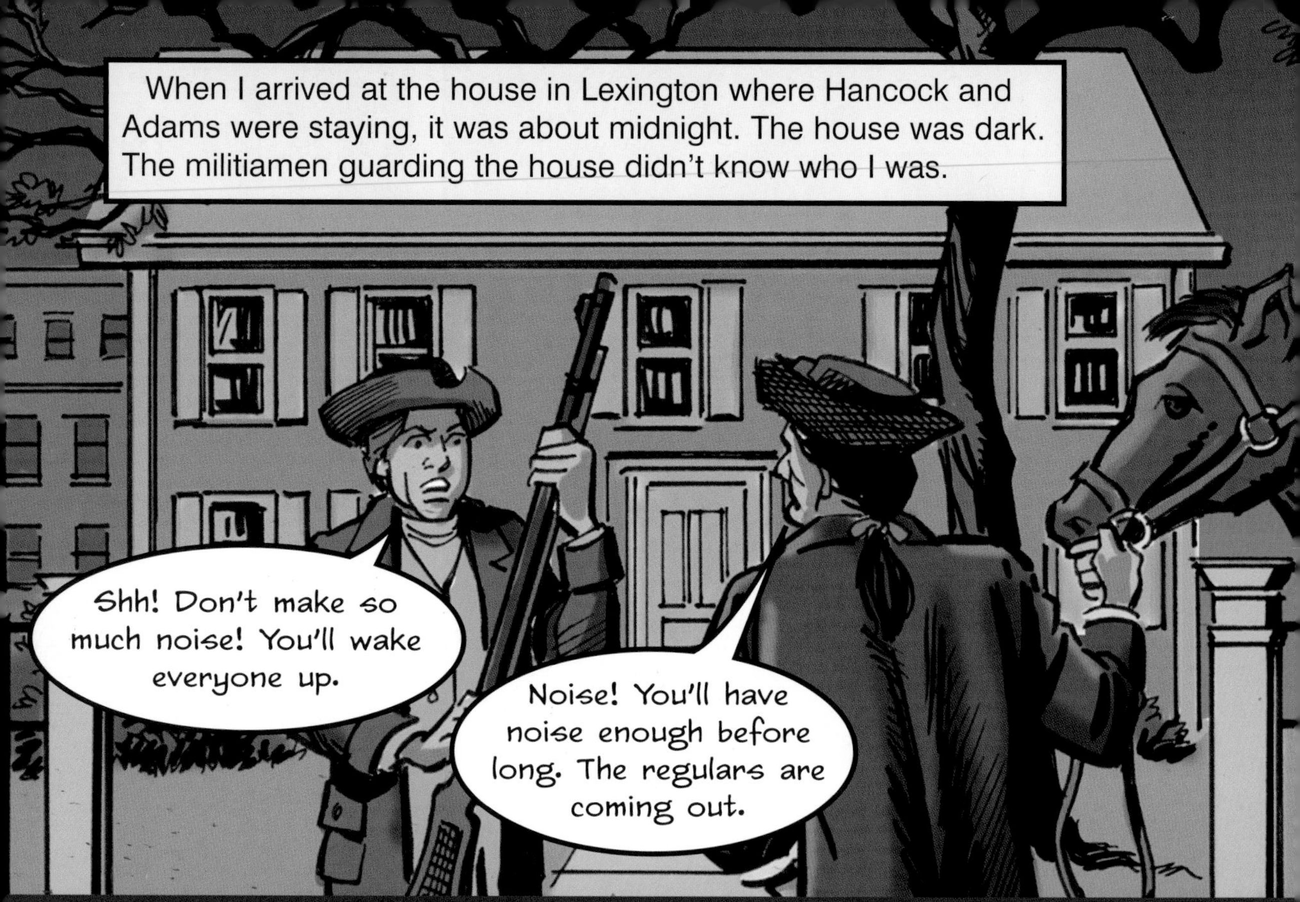
When I arrived at the house in Lexington where Hancock and Adams were staying, it was about midnight. The house was dark. The militiamen guarding the house didn't know who I was.
Shh! Don't make so much noise! You'll wake everyone up.
Noise! You'll have noise enough before long. The regulars are coming out.

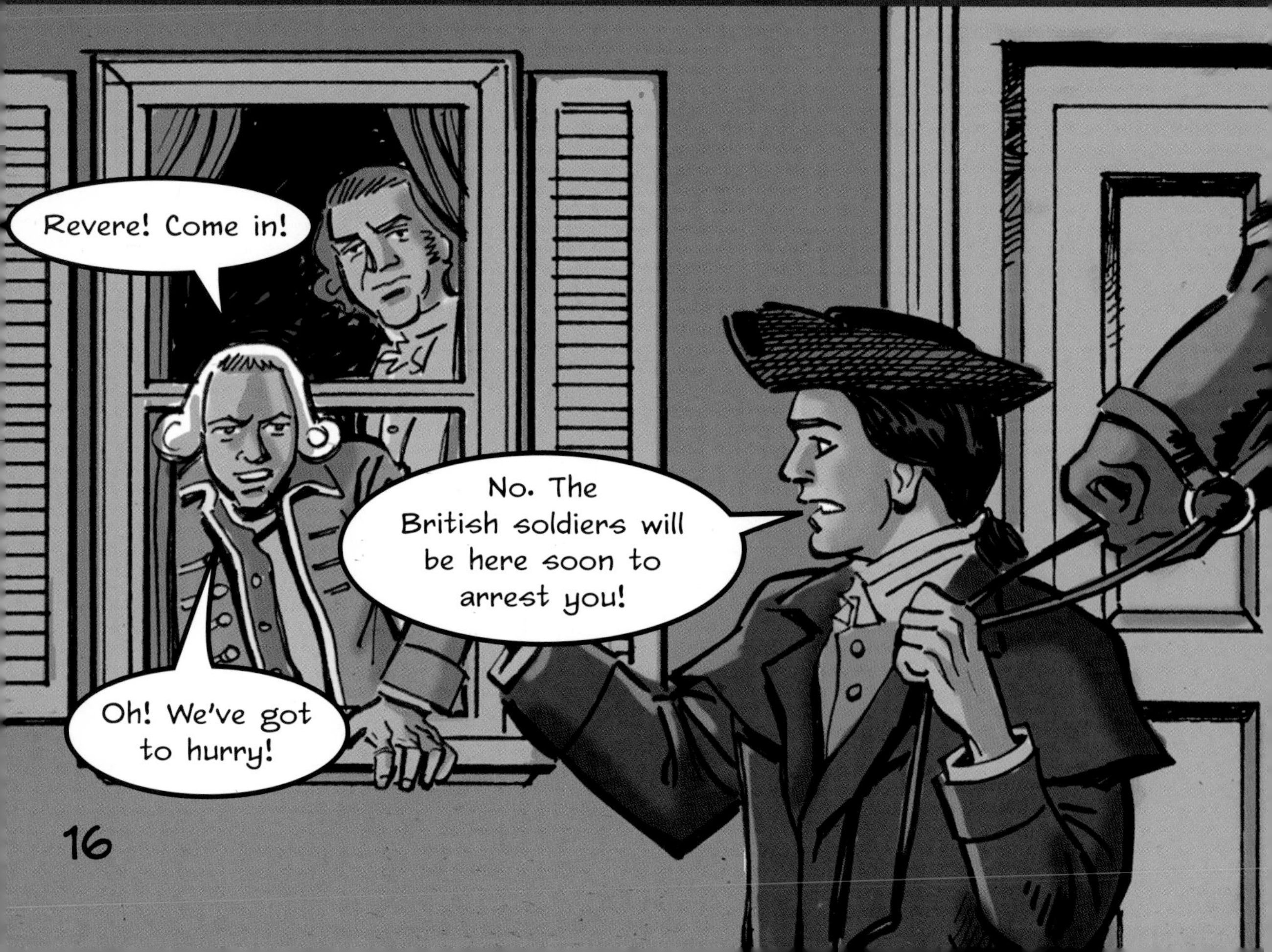
Revere! Come in!
No. The British soldiers will be here soon to arrest you!
Oh! We've got to hurry!

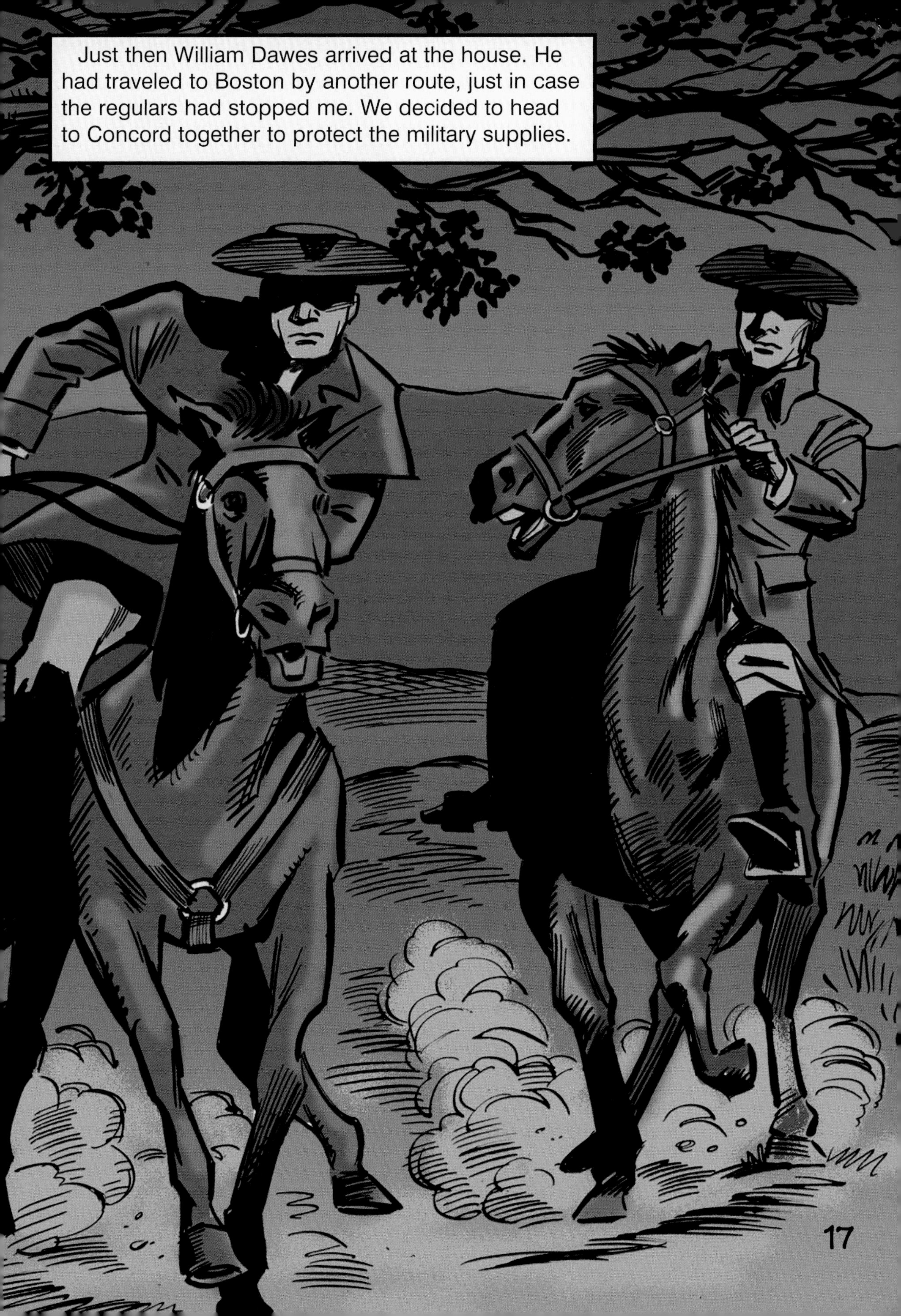
Just then William Dawes arrived at the house. He had traveled to Boston by another route, just in case the regulars had stopped me. We decided to head to Concord together to protect the military supplies.

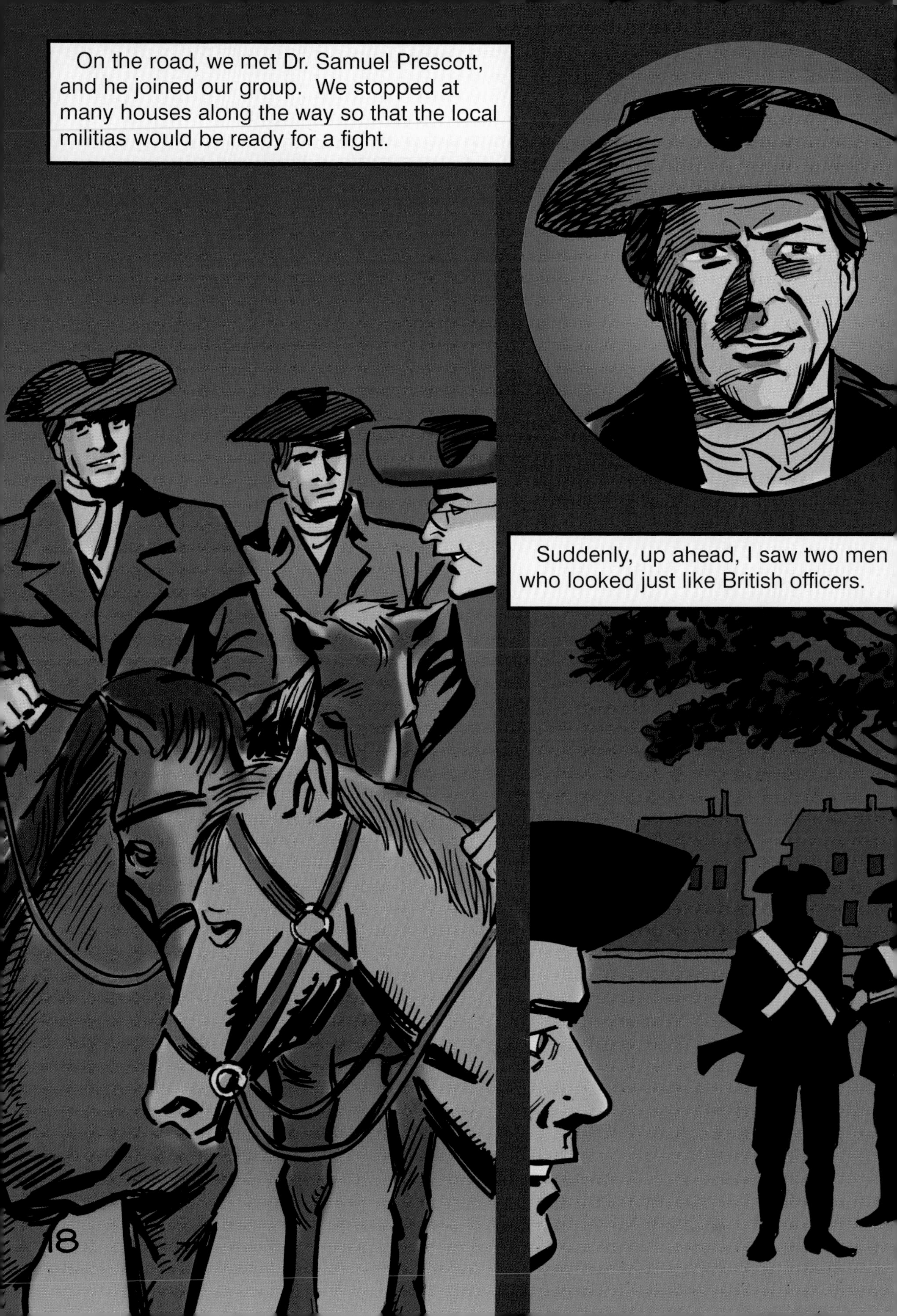
On the road, we met Dr. Samuel Prescott, and he joined our group. We stopped at many houses along the way so that the local militias would be ready for a fight.
Suddenly, up ahead, I saw two men who looked just like British officers.

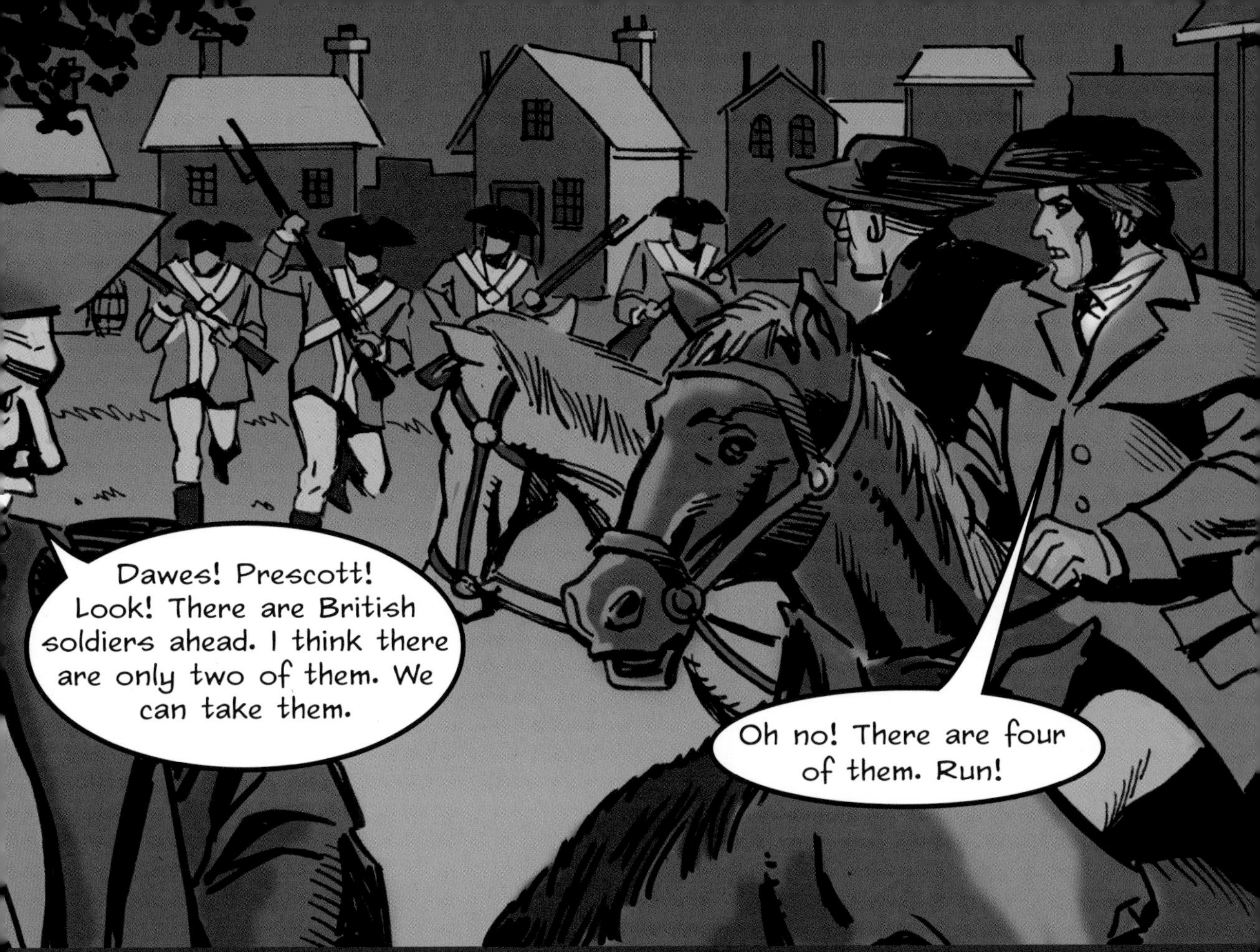
Dawes! Prescott! Look! There are British soldiers ahead. I think there are only two of them. We can take them.
Oh no! There are four of them. Run!

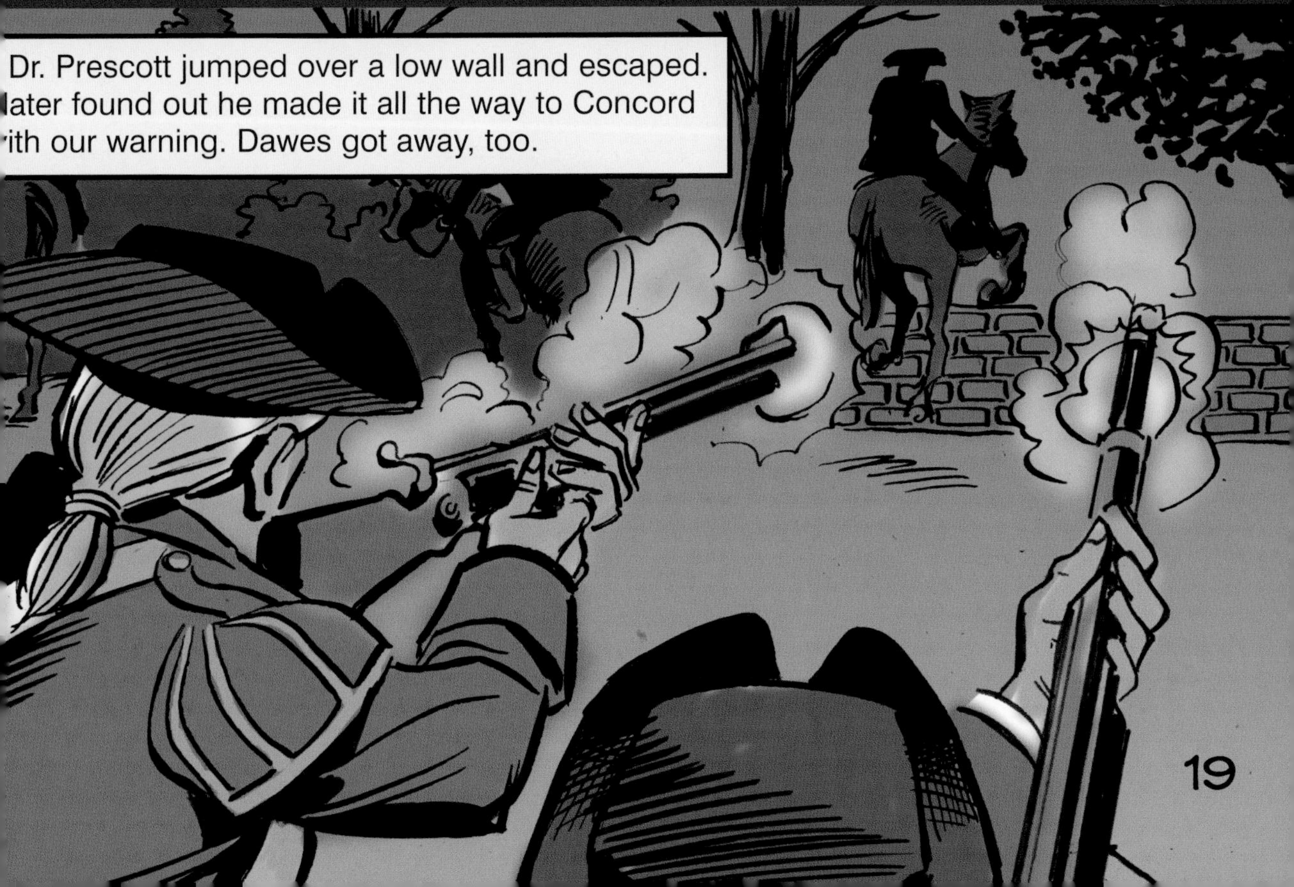
Dr. Prescott jumped over a low wall and escaped. later found out he made it all the way to Concord ith our warning. Dawes got away, too.

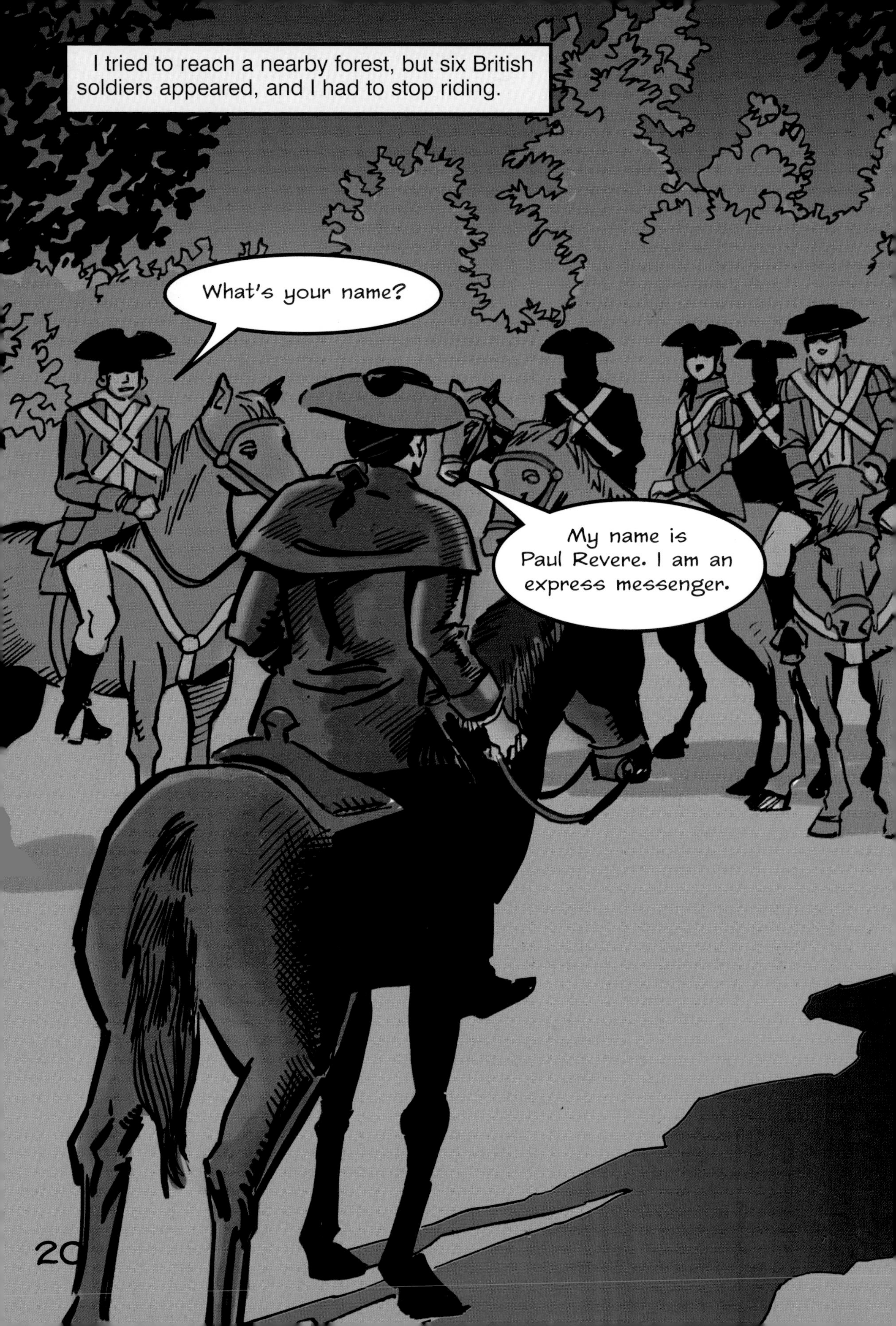

I tried to reach a nearby forest, but six British soldiers appeared, and I had to stop riding.
What's your name?
My name is Paul Revere. I am an express messenger.

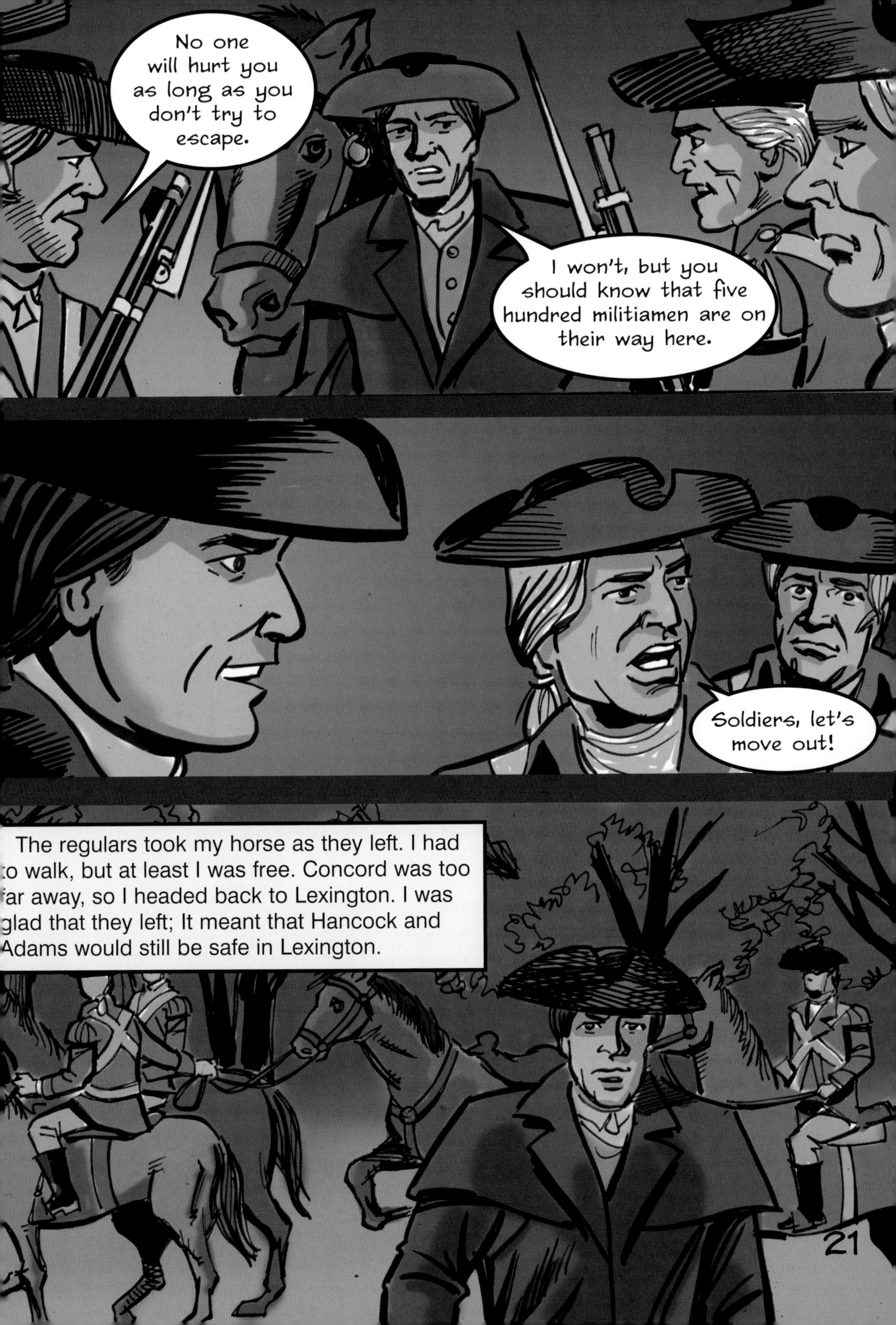
No one will hurt you as long as you don't try to escape.
I won't, but you should know that five hundred militiamen are on their way here.
Soldiers, let's move out!
The regulars took my horse as they left. I had to walk, but at least I was free. Concord was too far away, so I headed back to Lexington. I was glad that they left; It meant that Hancock and Adams would still be safe in Lexington.

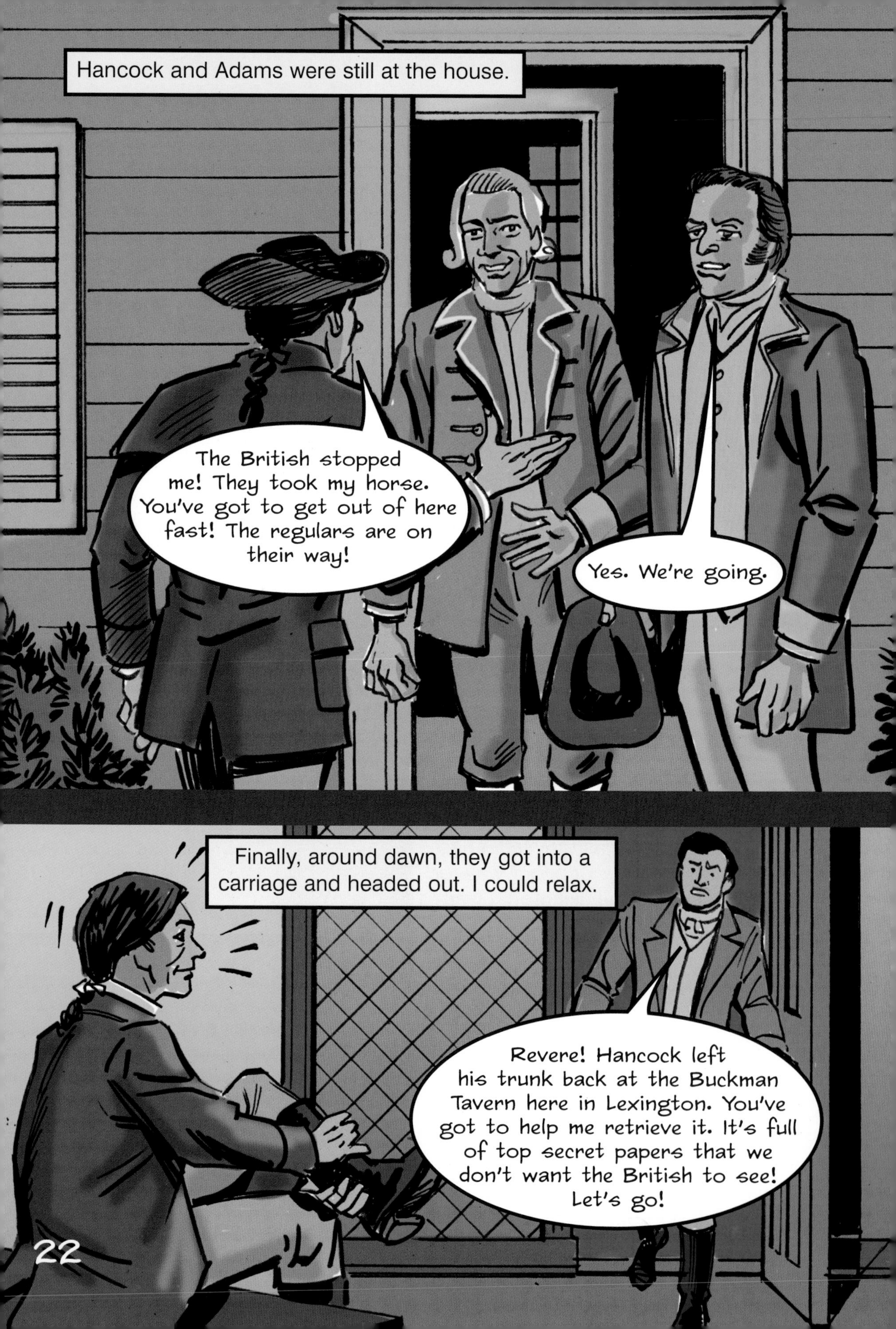

Hancock and Adams were still at the house.
The British stopped me! They took my horse. You've got to get out of here fast! The regulars are on their way!
Yes. We're going.
Finally, around dawn, they got into a carriage and headed out. I could relax.
Revere! Hancock left his trunk back at the Buckman Tavern here in Lexington. You've got to help me retrieve it. It's full of top secret papers that we don't want the British to see! Let's go!

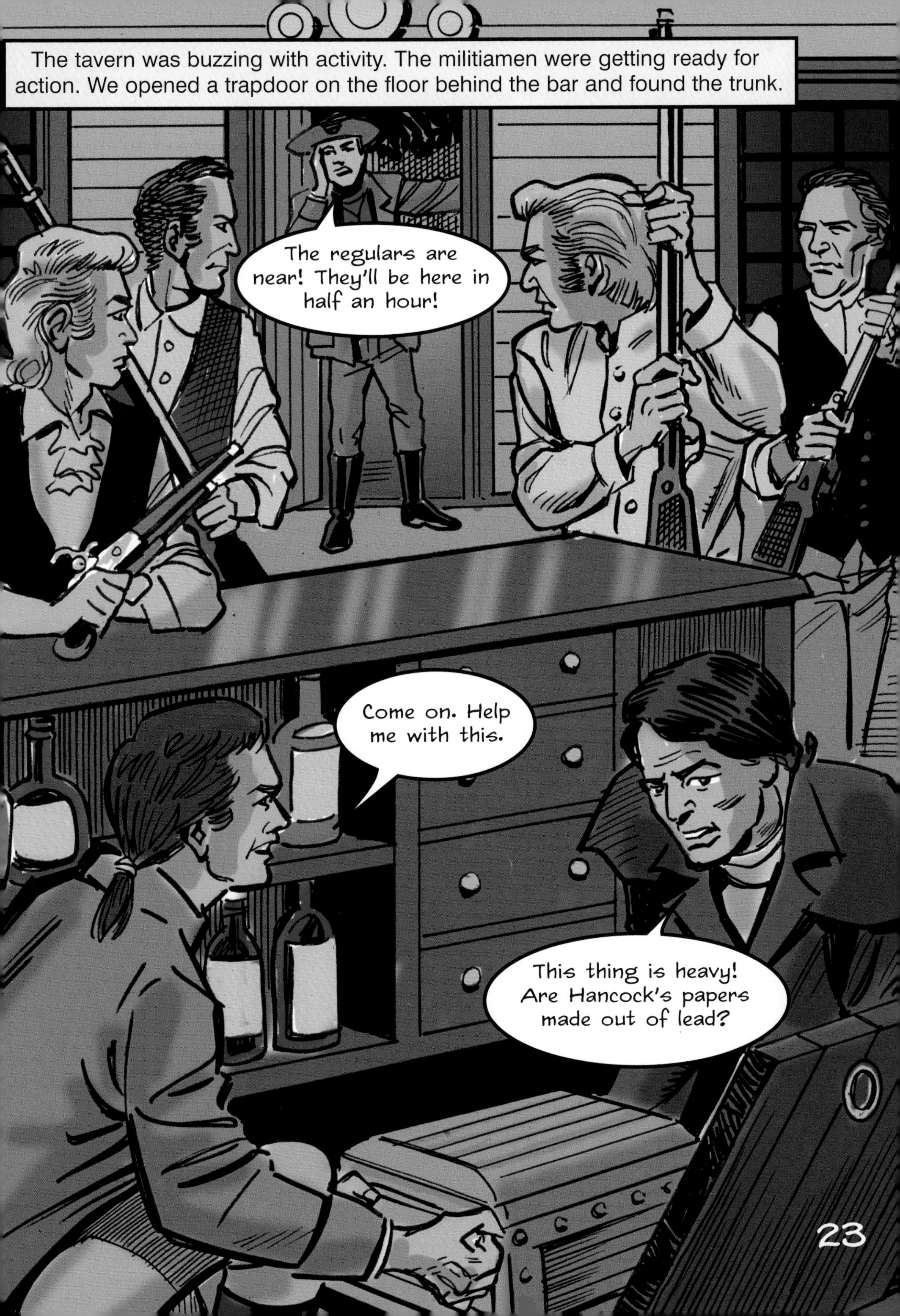
The tavern was buzzing with activity. The militiamen were getting ready for action. We opened a trapdoor on the floor behind the bar and found the trunk.
The regulars are near! They'll be here in half an hour!
Come on. Help me with this.
This thing is heavy! Are Hancock's papers made out of lead?

The Beginning of a Revolution

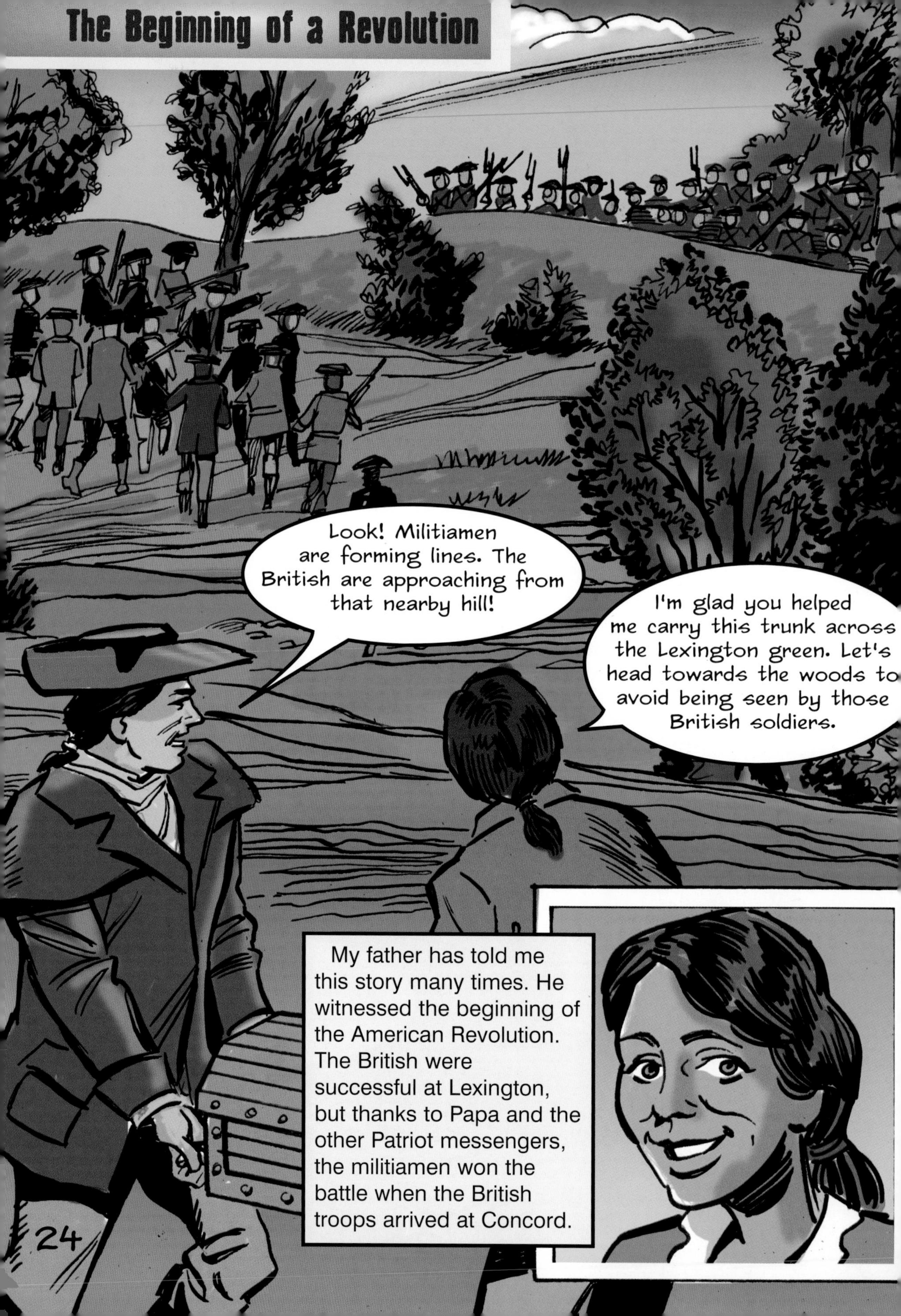

Look! Militiamen are forming lines. The British are approaching from that nearby hill!
I'm glad you helped me carry this trunk across the Lexington green. Let's head towards the woods to avoid being seen by those British soldiers.
My father has told me this story many times. He witnessed the beginning of the American Revolution. The British were successful at Lexington, but thanks to Papa and the other Patriot messengers, the militiamen won the battle when the British troops arrived at Concord.

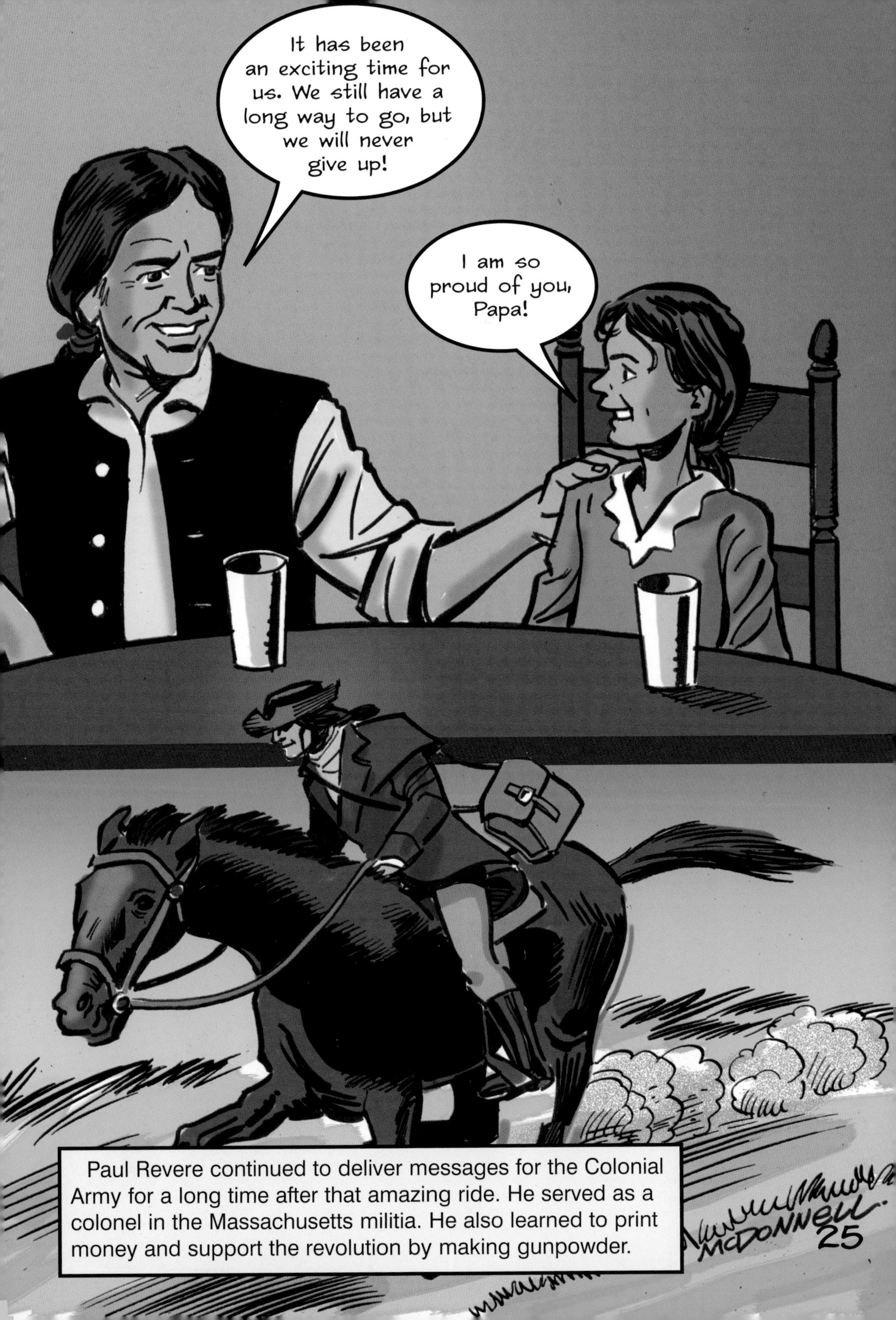
It has been an exciting time for us. We still have a long way to go, but we will never give up!
I am so proud of you, Papa!
Paul Revere continued to deliver messages for the Colonial Army for a long time after that amazing ride. He served as a colonel in the Massachusetts militia. He also learned to print money and support the revolution by making gunpowder.
McDONNELL

The Rest is History

During the American Revolutionary War, which is also known as the American War of Independence, the American Colonies fought to gain freedom from Great Britain. The war took place from 1775 to 1783, and ended with the formation of a new nation: the United States of America. About 25,000 American soldiers died during the war, many from diseases.

The American Colonies approved the Declaration of Independence on July 4, 1776. The Declaration officially declares independence from Great Britain and lists the reasons why the Colonies felt the British King had **violated** their rights. The Declaration of Independence remains such an important **document** in American history that we still celebrate our independence on July 4th, the date it was approved.

John Trumbell's famous painting, Declaration of Independence, *now hangs in the United States Capitol.*

Paul Revere's Ride

Today, Paul Revere is most famous for his ride on the night of April 18, 1775. He took a boat across the Charles River to Charleston, then rode through Medford, Arlington, and into Lexington. He made it part of the way from Lexington to Concord before he was stopped by British soldiers.

Listen my children and you shall hear
Of the midnight ride of Paul Revere,
On the eighteenth of April, in Seventy-five;
Hardly a man is now alive
Who remembers that famous day and year.
-Henry Wadsworth Longfellow

These words begin Paul Revere's Ride (The Landlord's Tale), a famous poem written by Henry Wadsworth Longfellow in 1863. This poem turned Paul Revere into a folk hero and a symbol of the beginning of the American Revolution.

Longfellow was a celebrated poet and literary figure in the mid to late 1800's. Although parts of the poem are inaccurate, many have found it to be inspiring and reminds them of what it means to be an American.

Lexington
Concord
Medford
Boston
Massachusetts

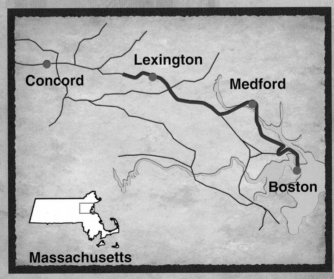

Today, much of the road Revere covered on his midnight ride is part of the Minute Man National Park. A marker stands in the spot where he was captured by British soldiers.

The Revere Family

Paul Revere had many children. His first wife, Sarah, gave birth to eight children, including Fanny, who was born in 1766. When Sarah died, Paul married a woman named Rachel, who also had eight children. He had over 50 grandchildren, many of whom lived with him.

Visitors can tour the Revere House on North Square in Boston, where the family lived for thirty years.

The Paul Revere House at 19 North Square in Boston has been open to visitors for over 100 years.

Paul Revere's Many Arts

Paul Revere was a skilled silversmith, but he also practiced other crafts. He made engravings on thin copper sheets that were then be used to print illustrations.

After the war, he began working with sheet copper for shipbuilding, and he learned the art of casting bells. According to an advertisement in the Boston Gazette, at one time he even made false teeth!

Did You know?

George Washington, our first President, led the Continental Army against the British. After helping the Colonies win the war, Washington became the first president of the United States in 1789. Paul Revere hoped to serve in the Continental Army under George Washington, but he was never able to.

Glossary

bellows (BEL-ohs): A bellows is an instrument that blows air onto a fire. Silversmiths like Paul Revere used a bellow to keep their fires hot.

colonies (KOH-luhn-eez): Colonies are areas inhabited by people from another country and still ruled by that country. The thirteen American Colonies that became part of the new United States were New Hampshire, Massachusetts, Rhode Island, Connecticut, New York, New Jersey, Pennsylvania, Delaware, Maryland, Virginia, North Carolina, South Carolina, and Georgia.

document (DOK-yuh-muhnt): A document is a paper that contains important written information or evidence.

militiamen (muh-LISH-uh-MIN): A militia is a group of citizens who are part of the military but fight only during emergencies. During the American Revolution, the Colonies didn't have a professional army and depended on the militiamen.

patriot (PAY-tree-uht): A patriot loves his or her country and is willing to defend it. During the Revolutionary War, the Patriots were people who fought for independence against Great Britain.

protest (pruh-TEST): When people protest, they object strongly to something. They might participate in demonstrations or sign petitions in order to express their disagreement.

representatives (REP-ri-ZEN-tuh-tivz): Representatives are people who are chosen to stand in, speak, or act for others.

revolution (REV-uh-LOO-shuhn): A revolution is a revolt in which the people rise up against their government to overthrow it or demand change.

silversmith (SIL-vur-SMITH): A silversmith is a craftsman who creates and repairs items made of silver.

tax (TAKS): A tax is a payment people pay to the government in exchange for defense, support, and services.

violated (VYE-uh-LATE-id): People feel their rights have been violated when they have been treated unfairly or without respect, or when a promise made to them has been broken.

Index

Websites

www.paulreverehouse.org

www.earlyamerica.com/paul_revere.htm

www.kidsandhistory.com/paulvm/_welcome.html

www.kidinfo.com/American_History/American_Revolution.html

www.pbs.org/ktca/liberty

About the Author

Holly Karapetkova, Ph.D., loves writing books and poems for kids and adults. She teaches at Marymount University and lives in theWashington, D.C., area with her son K.J. and her two dogs, Muffy and Attila.

About the Illustrator

Pete McDonnell is an illustrator who has worked in his field for twenty-four years. He has been creating comics, storyboards, and pop-art style illustration for clients, such as Marvel Comics, the History Channel, Microsoft, Nestle, Sega, and many more. He lives in Sonoma County, California with his wife, Shannon (also an illustrator), and son Jacob.

[redacted]